TAURUS

TAURUS

POEMS

PAUL NEMSER

new american press

Milwaukee, Wisconsin • Urbana, Illinois

n e w a m e r i c a n p r e s s

www.NewAmericanPress.com

Printed in the United States of America

ISBN 978-0-9849439-5-1

Cover photo "Minotaur at Athens Archeological Museum"
© 2007 by Dagrappler

Book design by David Bowen

For ordering information, please contact:

Ingram Book Group
One Ingram Blvd.
La Vergne, TN 37086
(800) 937-8000
orders@ingrambook.com

TABLE OF CONTENTS

ACKNOWLEDGMENTS

Many people encouraged me as I was writing *Taurus*, and many others helped to make this book possible. Thanks to all of you—publishers, editors, friends. To Andrew Hudgins for choosing *Taurus* to win the New American Poetry Prize and to Tom Daley for countless insights and close readings that helped the book take shape. Finally, I thank my wife Rebecca for her literary brilliance, sustaining enthusiasm, and constant love.

Special thanks to the editors of those publications where some of the poems in this collection first appeared:

Arion: "Ball lightning"
                      "Messages from the god"

Blackbird: "Attachment: Virtual matryoschka"
                      "Dream over dream"
                      "Foreword"
                      "from *The Scrapbook of Yevgeny the Robot Arm*"

Fulcrum: "The gargoyle's entreaty"

Horizon Review: "Europa's crossing"
                      "Visitation"

Pequod: "Bakery"

Finally, I'd like to thank the editors of *A Face to Meet the Faces: An Anthology of Contemporary Persona Poetry* (University of Akron Press), wherein "To the stockyard bulls" first appeared.

FOREWORD

A few years into the millenium, I was staying in a hotel in St. Petersburg, a converted apartment just off of Nevsky Prospekt. Mine was one of several small, steamy rooms around a shared bath. Each room had a single, springless bed and a tiny desk.

It was almost the summer solstice—white nights—and after tossing and turning in the light, I went down to the breakfast room for kasha and a hard-boiled egg. When I got back upstairs, I noticed that the door to a room near mine was wide open. The room looked as if it had been abandoned in haste.

Strewn on the floor were heaps of papers with Cyrillic writing, some typed, some in a hard, jagged hand. I started gathering these papers up, I'm not sure why. Since I didn't know Russian, I took some pages down to the desk clerk.

Shaking his head and shrugging, he translated slashes of handwriting: "Have city. Have bull. Bouncer—Rock Club Winter. Robot arms? What is this? Arms in love. Russian brides, radium watch dials. These are sold. Have movies, matryoshkas, personals. Borealis. Ball lightning. . . . Okay. Okay. Is good. A bull-gargoyle. Comes to life. Sometimes a god possesses him. A model. Mysterious. Name: Europa. Bull meets girl, and all Hell breaks loose."

Who hasn't ever wondered: am I a monster or is this what it means to be a person?

CLARICE LISPECTOR

The Hour of the Star
(Benjamin Moser translation)

Europa's crossing

**She dreams a
meeting.**

When I try to cross a border,
the moon is full.

I listen for footsteps.
Do they come for me?

I listen for eagles.
Have I reached the sea?

Antelope rivers
bound away into the firs.

Is that you, my bull,
crashing through tall stalks, my guide?

The clouds go fast.
Full moon, moonspray, no moon.

My fate steps forelegs
down out of the sky. My exile

beckons with shaken horns.
My husband bears me on his back

toward crosshatch birches,
where gods and men

walk in the same shadows—
walk with the raven and the wolf—

over snow cracks
of a dark imperium.

TAURUS WAKING

He returns to life.   Not far from Fontanka down a steam-hazed pinch
at a hidden turn in a little-walked street
is a building stranded in breathless depths,

once the home of a minor prince,
then apartments for titanium workers,
now a cavern—offices and shops—

behind a green façade that sprinkles plaster
when the summer moon
slices night like beets into concentric rounds.

That's when old women shout to keep cool,
and gargoyles—animal, bird, and every mix—
sleep in their niches, Taurus among them,

at peace, until the god is with him,
and metal softens, brackets give,
horns and fingers start to move.

His seized joints echo against the walls.
His first steps fail. He crawls into the light,
a metal man in the costume of a bull

hoisting himself up to his full height.
Hooves hit like iron on an empty street.
The city swirls, nightblind,

through museums for every kind.

Rain's erupting. He's had nothing to eat.

No idea what his heart may want of him tonight.

ICE CREAM

The bull-gargoyle watches a vendor in a park.

Look at the vendor's footsore, forward lean
to scrape a tub of *Keep in Shape Energy Ice Cream*
before an audience of squirrels.

Every hour he scoops. Squirrels dive after drips.
And neither they nor any bull can say what customers recall—
whatever streams, is wasted, sold,

skimmed, scummed, balls of sweetest bean or fruit.
Nothing outlives the moment it's seen. And seen,
and seen again. So the stars know

light's endless return as it comes around the curves,
nothing lost, just forever changed.
The bull watching, drowsily,

as the scoop forms layer upon layer.
Cow-milk lipids, free and bound, speak directly to his nose,
like a thickened cloud of kisses.

For seconds he loses the direction of time
as if the ball were forming in some rural back
when his foremost thought was grass and mother,

mother and grass and a blackbird.
And in that same scoop, he spots the flower of what's to be,
a tune he thinks he knows, or will,

or once lowed in giant, amorous bursts
to tangled, tender female wisps,
beauty out of cloud, the looking eye glommed

on a knee, white as an ice cream cone,
till all focus came apart,
and he could not say what he had seen.

Lightning's afterimage bleaches us blind, so we grasp
at stray scraps, a sprinkle, a fold,
as if gods' fortunes could be known, or animals' could be told.

Thus, a bull's fate is written on a match snapped afire,
phosphorus-hot, ephemeral desire
that cones up a ball of cloud

in the street where he was going, the milky street.
A body he's been, but there's a wring to his hump,
neck twisted back to see what's coming.

THE SIGHTING

Looking up from his soup, Taurus sees a rotating billboard, his first view of Europa.

Bull-gargoyle over a bowl of borscht
forgets for a moment that teetering existence
on a baroque roof, that uncomfortable

crouch, fixed, about to jump,
He pauses like one of those museum escapees—
actors, in period dress,

who pose for photos for a few rubles.
Their odd way of standing for hours, theatrical and pallid.
Their antique hats and collars

that frame the points and hollows of the skull.
But he's a god in the costume of a gargoyle
in a speed-shocked age,

antennae in his horns, mirror glasses.
He reads Roman letters from a scrolling placard—
photos of a model, her thick, open lips.

How palpable she is across land and water,
her dusky electricity
almost in his metal reach.

Synapses idling, he peers down into his soup
as if an undiscovered
dimension were curled up in the bowl.

THE CLUB

**Business life of
the bull-gargoyle
at the Club Winter;
nostalgias, trends.**

Floating by, a handbill: "The Past" and "Forget"—
"International Global Global Sensations."
Taurus will be there. He's muscle at the door.

Off the pedestal. A seasonal worker
at the club called Winter in sweaty summer.
The queue already reeking, standers who sell their places.

They jostle, smoke as if in a hurry,
talk about making it to another club's line.
Old people in the costume of pigeons.

The bull-gargoyle comes. They rustle,
get quickly out of the way. One can see
that he's a different order of beast than they.

In other times, they shared a meal
of leather belt, handfuls of peat, someone's pet parrot.
They wrote letters about each other, stole chairs for firewood.

But there is no market for pity, comrade.
Taurus's market's rising: crowd control, visas; export wives;
shares in a start-up radium outfit that will make the "Chernobyl,"

the cooling tower to be painted radioactive
on lead-shielded watchdials, a nostalgia item for anyone who misses
those cancer-bomb, luminous hands.

Informal economy

**Further in the
business sphere
of the bull-gargoyle:
brides, watches; two
robotic co-workers.**

Taurus takes a crate or two of watches for his "brides,"
whose photos lure traffic from Western men.
He pays the prettiest by the word

to excite the lonely, enchant them at viewing parties.
To the most productive girls, he delivers a watch.
They come to the Club in spectral paint, "RadioActive" tees.

Their dancing helps the take of the watch concession:
Chernobyl side by side with Aviator Paratrooper,
Flying Tank, Snowstorm Siberia.

The sales force is a multi-degree-of-freedom,
articulated, manipulator arm,
once telerobotic, with a speaker-independent,

natural language-based, voice-recognition interface,
now liberated as it moves through sales dances,
flipping and catching watches, passing the time.

Taurus calls it, "Yevgeny," "my cousin from Tomsk."
They've matched Yevgeny with a mechanical "Lyuba"
who glows green and seductive, flattering the alcove.

She charms tourists with tales of uranium,
powder the color of scrambled eggs,
named for the titan whose balls

became the goddess of love.

Swanlike, she glides along the blue concrete floor

behind Taurus's ticking wares.

FOUND: CLUB BILL—ENGLISH

BEANS (Neimegen, Голландия), ENGAGE AT WILL (Spb) и FUTURE DISORDER (Spb). Starts at 7 p.m.

24.00: Family Co. presents

2,9,16,23,30: KikabitZ invites: Evening jazz + live jams + pleasant evening program AND guests + **ENTRY FREE FOR GIRLS**

3: HARD SEXY HOUSE PARTY. Starts at midnight

4: SKAZY LESA

4,11,18,25: DJ, Re-disco, Solnechny Veter and guests (Classic Disco, New wave, CCCP retro). Starts at midnight

5: MASTERSELECTRODAY. Starts at 11 p.m.

6: MLAD I STAR

6,20: UNLIFE PROJECT «My House Is Your House». Starts at midnight

7: Pakava It.

8: MARZ PRO.presents: LONG-AWAIATED PRESENTATION OF THE X-TEAM ALBUM DRONAZ as part of the PERSONAGE-BIG JAM PARTY. Starts at 8 p.m.

24.00: Party by the company "Melody heart beats" Real grooves of Sunday

10,31: BASHMENT ALL STARS

11: KAMIKADZE

12: KOSHKIN DOME ELECTRODAY. Starts at 11 p.m.

13: MIZMA (Sweden, hardcore), SHADES OF GREY (Sweden, hardcore), DISTRESS (Spb, disk-core). Midngith: DeJa Vu.

Series of party dedicated to the legendary places of dance culture in St. Petersburg.

14: WASHING MACHINE. "Solar Project" group live

15: BROKEN RHYTHM DAY. R'n'B dance school from 6-8 p.m. 9 p.m.: TENGIZ RecordZ

    presents the party "READING HALL"

00 КикабитZ invites: Evening jazz + live jams + pleasant evening program AND guests

    + **ENTRY FREE FOR GIRLS**

22: THIS IS MUSIC presents: 8 p.m. NME PARTY post-rock (Lost Weekend — Moscow,

    Jumbo Jet, INFO). midnight: ONLY B PROMO

25: BESHENNYE OGURTSY.

27: BIG CITY GROOVES

29: Mozhzhevelnik (Moscow), (Moscow).

Midnight: LISTEN UP+ **ENTRY FREE FOR GIRLS**

EUROPA

The bull-gargoyle thinks about a model he has just seen on a rotating billboard.

Mind drifts to the placard's
beautiful rotation.
Even still,

she moves freely,
in fire.
She dances older newer

than the stars in Winter's cages.
Was anyone
ever so free to appear?

Her eyes humorous,
her forehead naïve,
as if she's

read
and forgotten
everything.

POMPEII

The model Europa
in her hotel room

I am a shape on the wall,
the searing on the wall.
When they come, they like to dress

my smiling shadow
who walks as I might
if rubber balls wore stilts,

melts as I might
if marble wedded H-bomb.
Soon enough

we are all quicklime . . .
Shockwaves flatten willows.
I am the daughter of a willow.

That one, by the Sarno,
the only tree,
only tree in the world for me.

They like to dress me
because I have an edge.
Turned edge-up, I'm vapor.

My hair like willow wands,
my S-curve trunk,
bounce

as a heat melts the dress forms,
the hangers, a bone-girl
made of wall and willow.

DREAM OVER DREAM

The bull-gargoyle, in St. Petersburg, imagines that Europa dreams she too is there; a boat ride.

Walking by Fontanka, I imagine you dreaming
that I see you dreaming on an evergreen bed,
and so we are together. It's night where you sleep.

Long past moonset, I rise behind mountains.
I climb them to look at you, fitful in bed.
You wonder at the brightness—only linked stars?

Nearly waking, but sleep ripples over.
A boat glides up with songs and flags.
Here is Fontanka. Here are the banks.

We board, haze-blind. The sinuous canal
wiggles vodka out of bottles, ghost boats in a dance.
At the back of the queue, ours pitches and rocks.

We duck heads under bridges, and fireworks explode.
I see nothing, love, nothing—infinite, daring,
your eyes, gray-green, the waters in them.

**The bull-gargoyle's
days on a roof, and
the leapers who
visit there.**

The gargoyle has witnessed enough for one century.
Felt cool accelerations on his cheeks—
for a lifetime, had he lived.

Hadn't frozen, goggled,
monstered about on his hind hooves,
consorted with the lower than low—

the mad ones, who hang around roofs, around ends.
Taurus knows intimately
the Spirit of the abyss, the raven-smooth,

tissue-thin, almost-ash abyss
whose wings generated wind
just below the bull-man

on moonless nights
when, sick of standing, Taurus wished
to take his mind off the scurryings on the street,

posturings of derelicts,
immensity of armies
desperate for an extra edible tuber,

and he lay down in a heap of nailed blond boards
pried up out of a palace dance floor.
He lay and let the moth wings

cover his unclosed eyes.
So tonight. There! Another sneaker clips the gutter.
Willing or clumsy, a torso goes over,

while Taurus feels the in-breath puffing his ribs,
then a gentle out-moo, as if he lay in clover,
pink, white, intoxicating.

"Everything alive is beyond help," says the bull,
witnessing the lost ones' cavalcade
through his grassy gaze.

Yet occasionally, he cheats the void.
A stray leaper tugs the bull-man's instincts
moments before a chosen launch.

At a peak of hysteria,
one of these roof-ghosts sees—a gargoyle?
Nodding, sympathetic as a priest?

She stops her muttered monologue, pets his horns.
When he touches her waist, she jumps back
from despair's dark hoop.

Taurus follows her for a brief seductive roll,
"before the great wheel
grinds us all for facepowder."

To the stockyard bulls

The bull-gargoyle addresses the bronze bulls who once stood by the gates of the old stockyard in St. Petersburg.

My bronze brothers, they cut exactly where our hearts were.
They knew us in the chutes and bellowing on blocks,

in wrapped paper parcels tinged with blood—
handed to women in chicken-print kerchiefs—

chewed in grand style by brush-bearded men in crimson vests
and long coats, who crumpled into chairs after dancing.

And here you are—tilt-headed, nostrils huge,
tensed to leap when there is no need to run,

having outlived the slaughterers and their house,
their long-tongued hounds lapping offal.

Trailered to the peeled pink gates of a former meat plant,
your bronze is more solid than the stage-set columns,

your legs more stout than the truck tires
heaped in squat, white-pink garages. Don't despair, brothers,

the gods ignite any and all. Some who leave streaks
like window water, others pent up in monumental pause.

They enjoy sitting inside us, ribbed bronze for a chassis.
In cool belly hollows, you'll feel a stirring

just as grass begins to push through gravel,
though your ears cradle gray-feather snow.

Yevgeny in history

1.   The Plutonian Years

**Background of
the arm; he
enriches plutonium.**

Mirage of a plant outside of Tomsk,
graphite-moderated, water-cooled.
Haze towers unnameable with human tongue.

Nonexistent complex in a nonexistent city
whose workers were not counted in any census,
and any flesh who traveled there

;

vanished entire—despite hot waste
excited in lake-sized pools
and rivers of electricity powering that latitude.

In that nowhere, I, a whirligigging arm,
received a name, "Yevgeny the arm."
I barely knew myself. I did not dream.

Yevgeny the mover, appendage to chemists.
They manipulated me from a shielded distance.
Who knew how far the isotopes would go,

to what distant vacation spot in America or China?
Not Yevgeny nonperson enriching nonplutonium
in Nowhere Siberia, arm of the state.

2.   The transportation to a happier plane

Transferred to the Radium Institute, founded by the genius Vernadsky, Yevgeny works on radioactive waste.

Ten-year plan done, they styrofoam Yevgeny,
 a silicon angel folded to the nth degree
of an infinitely small infinity.
They immobilize my chips. They immobilize my wrist,

just as a sawed-out violinist
has his floppy bow hand bound so he can sleep.

Soon, the crate nails howl.
Boards are pried open in St. Petersburg.

Here is the Radium Institute,
founder V. I .Vernadsky,
the great geochemist, the brilliant limnologist,
mapper of the radioactive flesh of Mother Russia.

Yevgeny full circle. Once "bomber," "poisoner,"
sponges up the Pu, U, and all the transuranics.

In pours the hot soup.
Moisture leaches out.
The loaded mineral block hardens.
I send the waste for storage underground.

3.   **Vernadsky!**

Cosmic energy determines the pressure of life that can be regarded as the transmission of solar energy to the Earth's surface... Activated by radiation, the matter of the biosphere collects and redistributes solar energy, and converts it ultimately into free energy capable of doing work on Earth... A new character is imparted to the planet by this powerful cosmic force. The radiations that pour upon the Earth cause the biosphere to take on properties unknown to lifeless planetary surfaces, and thus transform the face of the Earth... In its life, its death, and its decomposition an organism circulates its atoms through the biosphere over and over again.

Vladimir Vernadsky, *Biosfera*, 1926

I look forward with great optimism. I think that we undergo not only a historical, but a planetary change as well. We live in a transition to the noosphere.

Vladimir Vernadsky, The Biosphere and the Noosphere, 1945

The arm contemplates Vernadsky, whose unwavering vision led to the founding of the Radium Institute; Institute skills are put to many uses.

I stare all day toward V.I. Vernadsky
hanging on the wall where I work on sponge.

White triangle beard goes down the neck,
black circle glasses almost obscuring
the mountain range forehead, cirrus-cloud brows.

He seems to be looking right through the camera,
even as his eyeballs fall backward beyond earth—
outward and inward, Vernadsky's noosphere.

Years before anyone saw the blue spacy ball,
he seized the vantage point of god.

· · ·

From that now bald hill, I, Yevgeny the dutiful,
daily fill foam with waste.

Yevgeny the arm folds and straightens
to clean up the mess of making weapons and light.

I in a white room with shadows of Vernadsky,
near the optimist's photo and a list of goals in his memory,

bombarded, like me, by the forces of fission.
Deeds—what's their half-life? What is Yevgeny's

on the radioactive map in the radioactive hour,
in the moment of activity, in the hour of decay?

· · ·

Contemplating my half-life, I hit upon another,
doubled connectedness with the nervenets outside.

A janitor at the institute, for walking-around money,
has a side deal with a club owner on hot nights

to deliver dexterous and sociable robots,
dance-capable, economically canny,

on close terms with waste, radioactivity, and time.

FOUND: OBJECTS NAMED AFTER V. I. VERNADSKY

The name of the Academician **V.I.Vernadsky** is widely known not only in Russia but all over the world. **His name is given to**:

- State museum of geology (Moscow),
- All-Russian people's University for biosphere knowledges (Moscow),
- the library of the Sciences Academy of the Ukraine,
- Institute of geochemistry and analytical chemistry (Moscow),
- Nongovernmental Ecological V.I.Vernadsky Foundation, which instituted the Medal "For the Contribution to Sustainable Development" (1997).
- the golden medal and prizes in honor of Vernadsky (awarded by the Russian Academy of Sciences).
- Biosphere museum (St.Petersburg),
- students' sociological center "Noosphere" (Bauman Moscow State University),
- an underground station the *Vernadsky's Avenue* in Moscow,
- the station Vernadovka at the Kazan railway,
- a settlement Vernadovka near Simferopol,
- the research ship *Academician Vernadsky*,
- the steamship *The geologist Vernadsky*,
- an avenue in Moscow,
- an avenue in Kiev,
- the peak in the basin of the Podkamennaya Tunguska river,
- a volcano on Paramushir Island (Kuril Isles),
- glacial mountains in the Eastern Antarctica,
- a submarine volcano in the Atlantic Ocean,
- a new sulphate mineral "vernadite",
- a new species of diatoms,
- a mine in the Transbaikalian area,
- the crater at the back side of the Moon,
- a planetoid between Mars and Jupiter.

LOVE IN THE NOOSPHERE

Two robot arms,
co-employees
in the bull-gargoyle's
dance club, in love.

Lyuba and Yevgeny behind the watch table.
Her long neck, her virtual reality
man-machine interface

as she dances to the ambient and trance.
To his systems, she seems a green balletic swan,
given to desire infinitely,

given to desire with a precision
reserved only for utmost necessities,
the trimming of a tumor

around the optic nerve, a nanometer slice
from the jugular.
She barely touches the blue floor.

He longs to fuse his programming with hers,
to sweep with her through the wider arcs
neither one has yet known.

She turns her wrist his way,
offers her arm, her being, of her own volition.
He takes it, feels—alive.

The bull-gargoyle tormented by images of the model Europa.

It drives me mad—
these executions
of curve and tone.

I envy the photographers
who saw you live:
golden airy thinness,

a direct unceasing gaze
as if the lens had a soul.
But I see simulacra.

Colonies of starlings
flit and loop before me—
you on billboards, you onscreen.

Your language!
I sit at Кофе Хауз, coffee house,
near Gryphon Bridge,

on the phone, Телефон.
Molecules of coffee almost
glow up like embers in the stifled air.

I order "espresso."
I watch the scene.
Flying lions draped

with languorous lovers.
Snapshot. Snap. No haze, no shade.
Snap. Snap. Every shot rips a hole.

Is it like that for you,
my photogenic bird?
Lightbringer, when the shutter closes.

A BUS GOES BY

**The bull-gargoyle
sends a song to
Europa; her image
on passing buses**.

They've peeled back the skin of the bog
at a bulldozer site near the flood wall.
Black-backed gulls, feral cats.
One sopping dusk, I bring fishheads for all,

and a bus goes by. There you are on a phone,
in a striped T-shirt behind chrome bars.
Your geisha wince, as if sun never reached you.
"Locked in? No network? We'll give you ears!"

A thick-lipped man drinks vodka, peppered.
Three cats trail as I swerve between cars.
The man's empty bottle shatters near them,
outbursts of eye-cutting ice and stars.

Hydrocarbons overflow like milk
through the canals and past the park
where bear dancers whirl like holy fools
around a cub through the never-dark.

A bus goes by, and I'm anxious as a calf.
Now, in the shock of sun, I send you text
in the presence of the grid, in the presence of a god.
feeling your presence and the next

bus blowing by. Are you spirit, then?
Deep as a plunge off a sacred hill,
heart in flame like fire seen through rain—
so pale in brightness; in movement, so still—

or are you explosions of sycamores,
a circus contortionist's dance on her head,
the calendar's windows open to sea,
lanterns passing through homes of the dead,

an owl, barred by branches and moon
from flying to me, though I hear you call,
though you call all night, from far away
into my orifices, into my cell.

I slide through the mud handing out carp.
Rubs of light abrade my good eye.
Canals and terns. Headlonging love.
My coat drips. A bus! A bus goes by.

Personal ads from the bull-gargoyle's website for Russian brides.

Anna's personal info: I am calm and lovely. I have well-sided interests.

Wishes for partner: I want to meet a calm, intelligent and cheerful man.

His age: any

Angelina's personal info: They say I am feminine, tender, witty, sexual. I have very strong family values. I like to spend my free time in different ways. Everything depends on mood. Basically my interests are knitting, internet, cookery, sport, dances, and picture. I adore growing flowers. I like everything beautiful and believe that beauty will rescue the World.

Wishes for partner: I search a man, who would be strong-willed, hard-working, intelligent, household, purposeful

His age: any

Europa's personal info: Where are all the salmon? All in Kamchatka, with their pink eggballs and their windowing eyes. This is why I shall honeymoon there, mainly surrounded by ocean. I like the thought of pink flesh, tending to red. When I'm soft at night, not quite asleep, I listen for salmon in choppy streams of Norway. I lean toward the thrashing of salmon in the Loire. I burst through a dam and look for redds upstream in all the rocky sandy bottoms of Scotland. I open a can, put oils on my face. I tell the women's magazines the dams must go. And how I'll find the man who will bring me to Kamchatka when fins turn the water red as the bloodstream, and bears orgasmically slash at the birds who want their own salmon pie. And we will stretch out by a shallow stream, and volcanos will shake our milt-filled nights. And whales will mistake us for Steller's sea lions, rolling bigger than logs.

Wishes for partner: I seek a man with the angles of animals cut into his brow. A man who can go under ice, at the temperature of ice, find geothermal outflows, ride the lava as it falls to bottom. I seek a man for a valley of geysers.

His age: any

Tatiana's personal info: My friends consider me to be attentive and compassionate person, a woman who can help, who is a friend indeed, who is able to calm down. I think I am a weak and vulnerable lady though I bring up my son alone and make all manlike work alone considering home duties. I am a teacher by profession but I work in another field. Now I am selling the men's clothes, trying to give the clients taste to nice and fashionable clothes. I adore my family and try to make them the happiest in the whole world. My hobbies are my family. I like to spend time with my close ones. Often I spend time with my son; we are walking in the forest, in the nature. I enjoy listening to music both classical and modern. In my childhood I attended the musical school and learn to play piano. Sometimes I play piano for pleasure! I like making my home clean and cozy. I decorate it for pleasure. I adore cooking for my close ones... some tasty dishes and baking. My son adores cakes. In spite of the fact that I am a homely person, I enjoy traveling, exploring new places, cities and countries. I have a Siam cat at home. I like roses, blue cornflowers and lilies of the valley.

Wishes for partner: I wish to find a man who can find the approach to a child. My aim in life is to meet my beloved, with whom I will be able to spend my life and bring up my son! I dream about a happy and friendly family.

His age: any.

Europa's personal info: Rain comes. I separate from life. Sweet, absent light. What time? But I walk the better to think and be seen. A rat in a canal somersaults through my blood. My fur hat hangs low with moisture. Now I shall be seen by my love. I pass his security cameras, look into his lens, wave like a child to a three-block ocean liner. I play grand piano in a hotel lobby, where my love has eight wide-angle views of the leather chairs and the skinny palms that die and are replaced twice each winter. Sometimes I pretend to steal sevruga from a tray, or the score of Petroushka, or bauxite from a barge, so that he will know I think only of him.

Wishes for partner: I seek a man with high hopes and cheekbones. He must know all the parallel texts of his nature and must know who is roof to whom. We are all, after all, falling and rising in a house within a house, apartment in an atmosphere. We all have a place and an illness and a noose. It's important to get laryngitis, but keep talking. I want a man with insomnia when he comes to the beach and the sun's herd is restless, but he's supremely calm because he screens all the video, splices and snips, before he torches the spume at first light.

His age: any

Irina's personal info: I love children very much. I am very kind, friendly, faithful, and frank person. I am a person of humor and estimate friendship and good treatment to me. I like when a man can court a woman in romantic and beautiful way. I am very honest and estimate this trait of the character in others. I am very romantic person, so like the nature very much. To spend my time in the forest, to have the picnics, to listen to the birds, to observe the trees, to gather the wildflowers. I adore to be at the seaside and go to the beach. I like to boat. I can cook borsch and salads perfectly. I try to look very well and be in good form. I like cosmetics and perfumery. I am fond of travelling.

Wishes for partner: I want to meet a man with serious relations to me. I need a lot of attention, kind and warm feelings. A man must be very pretty, kind, with a feeling of humor, tender, he must estimate the beauty and share all interests with me. Sincerity and honesty must be the main traits his character. I want to be loved and one woman only for one man (height from 5'7").

His age: any

Europa's personal info: I am lively as a finch. I skate the edge of summer until I find it's winter, and then I am cold, but the sheep cuddle close. The geese huddle round, and I—I wait for love. It is the Fourteenth Century. Not far from Arezzo. Knights are making a pilgrimage in brightly checked robes. A reading priest walks into a tree. Greyhounds tear at a mole. I sip red wine, and it reddens my palate. Forehead dripping, I roast a lamb. I lay it over artichokes and noodles, drive away flies, and cover the food with clay and white cloth. I send it to my love, and it is spring. He writes a sonnet. On parchment, skin of a lamb. He seals it shut with wax of honeybees. "All for you," the package heavy with his ink. The letters illuminated. A drawing of me in fine lines curled into the letters. And the letters: his animal body, his animal eyes.

Wishes for partner: A man with a mineral strength. A straight-ahead approach. Who will breakfast on herbs and new-mown grass, his chest bare as a boulder. Whose words boom within that chest and Ohhhh comes out round as a sphere. A bull who outlasts another dawn, and another, and soon it's an eon of lasting. A bull-man in whom I have faith—with no faith himself, except the precipice. He is asleep now, standing up on a precipice. He opens his eyes and strides across rivers. He flashes across mountains, dives with dolphins, drinks down the Milky Way, outduels the Archer, jumps discordant into Orpheus's lyre, is honest and true, and false and ambiguous, double-edged, quartz-hard (shatters when you hit him in just the right place, so that sharp splinters shoot into your hand). He should be ductile in summer, labile in winter, and in all seasons, green. Perhaps he writes, as I peer over his shoulder: "I looked into St. Augustine's *Confessions.* Where I first fixed my eyes it was written: 'And men go abroad to admire the heights of mountains, the mighty waves of the sea, the broad tides of rivers, the compass of the ocean, and the circuits of the stars, yet pass over the mystery of themselves without a thought.'" I am looking for such a man.

His age: any.

ATTACHMENT: VIRTUAL MATRYOSCHKA

**An email attachment
in which the bull-
gargoyle imagines
Europa as a nesting
matryoschka doll**.

There are as many foreign objects
on earth as in the sky,
a paradoxical finding.

All these divisions—
space into time chambers,
time into space!

And I have come to see perfection
in all forms is divisible,
high or low, deity or dust mote,

even you,
my perfect many-in-one,
and so I have had made

this matryoschka of you,
of captured impulses
and sparks.

You inside you
and inside that
is you,

child-sized you, fingernail you,
the tiniest speck
without flaw.

STROLL

Taurus the bull-gargoyle, inhabited by a god, takes a walk with Yevgeny the robot arm.

"Never been a morning like this," says Taurus.
"There's never been this morning," says Yevgeny.
"Many are like, one identical,"

reading from his instruction set, which does the thinking.
Taurus has no instruction set. Only the god.
The god commands. Taurus does.

The god instructs. Taurus fights, learns.
His bronze legs creak like birds in their hip housings.
Corroding, Taurus is unlike the god

who moves morning to morning in a streak of bronze,
bull-fast, puffing and procreating.
This morning the god calls himself "Taurus." He says:

"Never been a morning so swift or so new—
now red-sun pools are steaming,
and mushrooms are learning to eat metal."

Taurus and Yevgeny stroll under morning firs,
bronze bull, robot arm squishing spongy ground,
the fungus under all.

Yevgeny's birthday address

**The robot arm's
first scrapbook
entry.**

O the energic mechanisms, my friends,
the rivet and the joint!
All is fixed, but has a pivot.

I cannot speak to you
but in the language you've given me.
And therefore on my birthday

as on the dawning day of "dawn" and "day,"
your interface faces mine
when I turn toward you,

and with a wave of my very arm,
I blow out beeswax candles
manufactured on visits to how many roses,

each one waving stem—an arm,
blossom—a hand,
each one having said, as I do—I am.

Yevgeny's reach

**The robot arm's
credo.**

Maintain a small footprint, citizens,
a small footprint.
Be small where you anchor.
From there, unfold.

Like arms of the wind, reach through branches
to shake the petioles
at the orange brink.

Every stretch has a starting point.
Every mound is a mountain.
Before the world was matter, a ray stood up.

Up—and then it moved.

Chips by night

**The robot-arm's
chips meditate,
activate; his eye.**

It's the cobalt hour when waves
float like stitches through phosphorescence.

Sparks, once born, die faster
than we can catch them in our nets.

Moon's hand ladles the sea into a bay.
Wind's hand spatters it out as spray.
A comb of stars parts the dark.

We're alive as kelp or krill, though we're alloy and resin,
silicon, copper, acid, flame.
In our caves of sand, currents flow and knit.

An eye sees the lab. The eye of Yevgeny
sees a square of moonlight pour through like seawater,
over the still hand.

Hand

The robot arms'   Hand the Creator made all out of nothing,
creation myth.   pushed back the night a fraction of a whir,
made owl out of—mesh out of—man out of—nothing,

where they'd sloshed in formless dislocations.
Hand lifted them out of the darkling womb.
They were butter sopping from a churn.

Hand the Creator had a hand with a hand,
in all an infinite adding of hands.
They assembled the world in no time. . .

Out of beaks and night's hair, mouse necks and rain,
crows' windless ambushes, gnats' cloudy massings,
miracle of who-ing in the mesh of night,

out of whom, says the man, says who, says the owl,
I, signs Hand, pointing like a beak
punching rows and columns of stars.

Parable of the components

The god of the robot arms conceives their components as birds.

Hand the Creator wove birds upon birds,
and thus there were always wings in the air,
there was always nesting and feeding.
Here was a bird, landing in a birch,
there another bird hymned on a branch.
Hand scooped up songs that came off the branch
and wove them into birds upon birds.

Yevgeny's paradox

The robot arm takes his first breath.

The best rule is known from what follows,
best forgotten in what follows.
A rule's desire is best known in violation.

I am a robot arm. I cannot breathe.
My Ruler: "Yevgeny, do not breathe."
And I breathe. In terror of suffocation.

A letter in another hand

The robot arm has saved a letter from his beloved, another robot arm; here is the letter.

I can't stop sighing. My compressor's never full.
I'm a binary being in a bliss of rules!
The humans are sympathetic. Kindly mouths
deform across their mandibles like honey down a wall.
But they give me green feathers and an alligator glove
when I crave algorithms, oil, and lightning.
We, my love, are in sequence, in phase—
ting and ping, the thunk of purpose.
White herons' long-legged mazurkas through mallows.

Yevgeny's daydream

His reverie: the biosphere.

The grace of wheat grains broken from a stalk.
I have no need of these, yet I love them.
Rain would set me sparking and shorting,
but I rejoice in its irregular tap.
Husks, toenails, lost mitochondria
soften in a stream among salmon skin and milt.
Pathos of a softer world.

Yevgeny's homesickness

The robot arm,
who came from
Tomsk and now
works in a
St. Petersburg lab,
contemplates a
carcass.

The dead winter squirrel in the driveway;
by summer a fluff-puff gray tail.

The forepaws, taken up by a tire,
now spin through Siberia.

Drop an acorn by my home, little hands.
Drop an acorn there for me.

Yevgeny's letter to Lyuba

The robot arm
answers his beloved.

You've undone me.
I have given up the Eden
in my gears' mindless meshing.

Yevgeny thinks of insects

**The robot arm's
affinity for insects**

I have learned to play instruments
without tapping a foot.
Action's best confined to needed motion, as a seawind
brings only the necessary squall—
big enough to sprout a lettuce seed.
An ancient voice locked in a human voicebox
calls to me in songs of grinding stone.
Scratches and quakes! I can barely understand.
The garden is green because
the infrastructure has not reached it.
Today, more cricket than man,
I long to walk in dirt
and macerate a rootling,
to lock on a mate and make larvae, every second to an end
unfogged by many selves,
to be gathered around a single, small "i."
I am an arm. Armness enlivens me.
Is it so much better to be glorious,
chasing grand uses in the feral twilight?
You humans walk eyes half-closed into night,
feeling for a tingle, a respite.
There's less air each time you breathe in.
My six-legged soul wouldn't bend a grass blade.
Through my carapace
I'd bathe in little winds.

Yevgeny's praxis

A call to arms.

Do not be eager. Do not be slack.
There's no way without work.

This room's a desert.
Pack along, bounce over a rut.

Moments are meteors. Look:
A finger streaks the dark!

Yevgeny's faith

There is permanence in repair.

PHASES

The bull-gargoyle thinks of Europa as having different phases, like water or the moon.

She is the fall wave that fetches boats up
on the Peterhof beach
when gulls hunt herring, rococo fountains loop,

and the princesses' peasant palaces
are feverish for glints
against the scalloped fish-gray of the bay.

She's a gated garden bordering a "Greek" temple's
gray, scalloped pools.
She's the white bubbles where water returns

from its airy arcs and cataracts
till fall collapses, vibration slows.
She's a groan on a darkening road of bones.

A railroad arrows the steppe in the throat.
Hands that stanch the bleeding
shrink to sticks, freeze as hooks.

She's the delicate bones in a broken foot
that walks and walks as ice collects ice,
numbing it, numbing it.

She barely leaves a print, yet she's liquefying there
as earth opens. Borders change.
She is watercolor sinking into paper.

She drips beyond the edges, the drips now a stream,
stream's a torrent, the torrent dives.
She curls into chambers, hissing on magma.

A vision of Europa as the soul of magma.
Taurus has never witnessed such excitement
silhouetted in steam.

SCARLET SAILS

School's out.   When there is no night, the night crawlers

burrow even deeper
in the seepy loam.

When there is no night, the old looms

clacker at the new ones;
and silk falls like a river.

When there is no night, I look for you.

I find scarlet sails,
the slippery decks.

We cannot—almost—almost drink—all night amid

the fireworks' chatter, saying

free will's inescapable, and night is love's victim

(under halos of white birds and sodium lamps,
under brightening empires of slash and strike,

daffodils igniting in stratus.
O how much we drank!).

Sleep has no future when there is no night,
though bridges pass above us,
a brief gift and grief of night,

the hull a tympany irregular as hearts,

while spidery boats throw their silks upon the waters,
and the waters
wear them as night.

Touch this coppery skin, love. It is the skin
of the broken, of regiments
corroding in snow. Skin
of the saw's teeth, cutting as it saves.

Though I sink like the sun into a stand of pines,
though you turn to leather and I to sea,
be my sand, be my salt, be the shaking

that knew me
when there was no night.

Europa declaims

Europa anticipates what she might say upon meeting the bull.

I'll play any part. I'll be a shovel.
I'll spread manure on banquet platters
and smear your temples' pitted steps.

Murderers may sleep soundly beside me,
but I'll dig up their wine-rich hillsides.
I, who can't be gripped or thrown away,

will beguile with paradox.
Like this: the terrible is never new.
To be terrible, it must have known us

when we trotted four-legged.
When I meet you, my terror, I shall know you.
I am an actress. You are a bull.

Let that define us. I'll be a cow. You are a god.
If you do not want beef,
then milk me for bone.

If you do not want my milk,
I will calve for you,
and our children will pillage and plow

by the Aegean, by the windy cliffsides
of Apennine and Caucasus.
We shall teach them not to eat their own kind.

Nature to the Gargoyle

The bull-gargoyle
inhabited by a god
considers nature.

Nature perplexes him.
His very being denies it.

O god, O bull,
twice profane.

If he saw the innocent
carried away, herded away,

given away,
he was not torn apart.

Bronze hide clung
to bronze heart.

When he looked upon
teeth-taped-shut reeling orphans

lined up at
psychotropic dispensaries,

he merely wondered if the snow
on his nose would gain a cm,

or melt and refreeze
in a blinding glaze.

Brutal metal, a hollow bull
has no moral nature.

Yet for a bull-man—
habitation of a god—

the delirious laughter
of sea slapping pine,

frozen winter waves
in spring collapse,

the origami heart
unfolding in a peony

perfuming the Bay of Finland,
nature echoes

through his infernal temples—
his minerals, filth, lava tubes,

the fumaroles in the folds
of his tarnishing thought-field—

it all seems dandelion-
bright right now,

past saying for an ungulate
of bronze.

Europa's monologue

She imagines what it will be like to think back on meeting the bull.

Every breath is danger.
The bellows says *I know. I know. I know.*
One morning, the sun's a tangerine, the next
black bread ballooning.

Stickiness of memory, an icon's tempera,
animal glue and honey on alder.
I knew you once. I was bark-hard then.
Just born of seed, and branching.

That is when gods come to us
dressed in hide or wings.
Their beaks pinch foreheads.
Their hooves X our sex.

You were horns, or a memory of horns.
I prayed to your blackness.
It could have been whiteness.
Like every clarity that comes from god.
Like every past where gods are ambered
in animal glue and sap.

This is the reason all planes fly backward:
In other times, bulls were not simply bulls
to be studied on scientific principles.

Girl and bull and the dizzy moon,
a pasture's lavender smithereened.
Drunken temples, cartwheels in torchlight,
Ring-dance of girls, alder-green. . .

Now in casinos, I roll and roll.
Every tick risks a future.
Every outbreath's a kiss.

And I lose the makeup on my mask, find
blubber and bone.

This is why everyone
falls off:

My mother on the carousel horse at the front.
My mother on the carousel horse at the back.
A barebacking Cossack rides the roulette wheel.

This is the reason
all planes fly forward.
I know. I know, know, know, says the bellows,
when all it thinks, all it knows,
will be fire.

Hermitage dances

1.   **Dance among snowberries**

The bull to Europa.   From among the circle in the great Matisse,
you twirled out naked, feet in snow.
The bull, shaking his balls, rakes ground ice
melted wet where you stepped.

2.   **Dance of the lapping Neva**

Every river undulates thousands of times.
Only the first is innocent.
But let the wave of your hair unbind,
fall free again and again.

THE GARGOYLE'S ENTREATY

The bull-gargoyle resorts to formal argument entreating Europa to accept his love.

Oblivious to the hearth
of this aging icy world
where all that moves is death,
I slumbered in fire's mold.
I hardened in a shape.
Tongs yanked me from the mold.
They dropped me near a pipe.
For months I slept in ash.
My only dream was sleep.
Ash came off with a brush.
A file scrubbed off my burrs.
A ballpeen was my lash.
I was the sum of scars.
I was a clapper's crash
for gods and revelers.
Function hammers form.
I stand upon a roof
and witness. There's a swarm
of human bees, a cough
of little fates. A worm
spins out a perfect life,
ennobles to a saint.
He's eaten for a laugh.
Half of all deeds are lint.
Half of all hopes are spoils.
One tries to wash. One can't.
Loose love pours balms and oils.

Love is the end of one.
Love is for gods and fools,
for wire-borne girls, alone,
for sack-borne sperm that crawl
till genes' extinction,
or even for a bull
occasionally alive
when god delivers all
and unities revive
as body, mind, and soul.
This is the laugh of love:
It starts down in a bell.
It starts down in a shoe
and rises in a wail.
It lavas in the blue.
It heaves a trembling tail.
And then one dies in two,
and two may fuse in all,
for god makes one anew.
Then be with me and roll.
Let my blood play in you.
Sweet myrtle's pressings heal.
There's nothing death can do.

NUCLEAR

**Europa dreams
that she is lying
with the bull-
gargoyle; love
as a nuclear test**.

I don't believe in silence, but I started there.
I believe in moons irradiating clouds.

But here, as I dream this,
you sleep in me,
and we in desultory dew.
What's bigger now, this cloud or you?

Come, we'll sleep when all's exploded.
Let's rise and split and slice like moons.
Eclipse me. Reflect me
in a broken reef, a blackened sea.
I'll destroy you if you destroy me.

Does death hold any shape at all
between parentheses—your horns?
I've heard that every baby mourns
when she sails the long canal.

Standing up on spindly fours,
were you mourning too?

Were you once a calf? I've always been a child.
I've desecrated borders, fieldstones, walls.
I've trampled where the sowbugs wailed,
and even now, keep company with girls
who herb me like a roast, and slather rocks with oils

and glide the rocks around my breasts,
the softest hindpart of my knees, and tell me what exists.
They teach me vowels to say to boys,
pour yogurt in a bowl

and swirl in clouds of mint
until I'm reeling from the smell.

And they talk to me of pasts,
but never of a bull,
when all I plan about, and pant about
and launch for is a bull.

Bring me spoons then, bull-man. Bring me suns.
I believe in steps, but I don't believe in stones.

Let's make a Braille of mushrooms,
raze each forest, town, and hill.

Come to me in the terrible night,
in the fallout's terrible drool.

Then Come

1. The bull's humility

A seduction.

A dust-scorpion runs from hiding, but my hoof beheads it.
I put the spiked tail in a tumbler of vodka, and we drink.
To the limitless gods who have graced us with defenses!
But you've no need to fend me off with hand or tongue.
I lower to the steppe, smitten—onto your petals, your pyre.

2. Meeting

**The bull-gargoyle
tells Europa how
to find him.**

Were you left behind when everybody fled the last century?
Remember how you planned at the age of six to be a planner, to serve
and report, report and serve, with all the clean elegance of a gate that locks?
You still know the way to that gate, without directions or footprints.
You know it like fresh air and foam, like dill and black pepper.
Just as I found it one day in the labyrinth,
and parted your latch as if you were the monster.
You before you knew it was you. Look for me there.

3. Knees

**The bull-gargoyle
speaks of her desire.**

Look there. In that fire.
In the blue

that curls and spits in the alderwood,
you see horns.
You see haunches
formed in the spicy smoke.

How then do I stand on the beach before you,
a bull, solid and white?

On white-hot hoofs that boil
the salt flood wetting your knees.

4.   Knowing

The bull-gargoyle tells Europa that being with him will bring her knowledge.

I will speak to you of things known only to the god.
How do I know them? Because he is with me.
How remember? He does not strike them from my mind.
Why am I not soundless, like a bell his hand has quelled?
There is a girl, sincere as a siltless creek,
generous as a hot spring shallows,
the shape of a goddess god-made for passion
like a mix of clay and glass red-heated on Olympus
and motorcycled to this room by the Winter Palace,
a back room in what was once a stable,
there to cool perfect as a shadow of a pear,
to ripen in the darkness that swells in these walls.
The secrets I will tell her, the ways she will give in,
as we glide ever deeper, room by room,
and every key I show will tell all about its keyhole.
All of her doors and all the spaces
will know the mercies of the many-fingered god.

VISITATION

Europa's dream.

I hear a wave, angular and wet.
Only one wave.

It is a sea, though I sleep in mountains.
One come alive.

How did he come here, the one I awaited?
Changing rain.

Bull, my only, other-than-earthly—
Soul-heavy stone.

Sing, as to women you knew before me.
So many gone.

Ring for others who'll follow my shadow.
Now but one.

I lie among loss, and ruin, and glaciers.
One torch, one cave.

This is my answer to layers of sorrow.
Ululate love.

The sea snows. The snow I scoop from waters—
This one place.

Melts on my palm. Oh! Love's weather!
One mingled race.

WINTER

Europa sends
the bull-gargoyle
a note describing
her visit to his
dance club, Winter.

It is 45° C, and I'm wet as a doe
who's run the first week of a months-long migration.
Your Club is Winter. Dark as a sleetstorm.
It is black and white and soviet brothel.
I shudder out of the lift like a contraband snow leopard
unloaded from a steel mesh box.

The sealskinned girl behind the counter
hands out baby herring on a silver tray.
Two drop headfirst onto my tongue—
out of the arctic, for me.

The bartender's vodka almost freezes to my hand,
In the half-light, the vodka is blue as nightfall
when trembling atoms damp their hum.

I've never been so awake.

Something beats, bonestick on drumskin.
I'm traveler and journey, carcass and grail.

Tundra in a maelstrom, dancers flap,
then hover like dust above torn, dry grass
after caribou have come through.

I trace their hopeful transits around the Pole.
Like snowflakes in snowflakes, they break.

We come to a cubicle. You pull shut
the black kimono cloth, and it is darker still,
Only a miniscule Ursa Minor
claws through the northern ceiling.
And there in the center is an icebed,
prairie-huge, bounded by pine boards,
whitened by vast linens,
the linens overlain by plats of mink
strewn with goldenrod and paintbrush,
tundra swans for pillows;
at each of the four corners, a white wolf.

You calm them
with a shake of your horns.

Then the only sounds: ice building, melting,
sough of grass on lazy grass,
the ocean's distant lap, lap,
stretch of outspreading lichens.

I tell you that I have read about these freezes.
I have heard that the starving can scavenge for days.
I have seen swans and wolves
on a lacquer box night
when I was a schoolgirl—unformed,
one thing, not yet many,
and I needed a dream to ravel me.

"This is love then," you say,
as I surround you in your night,
all the minerals, the ledge ice, the mirror-break seas.

When I leave the Club, I look for the North Star.
The city's 4 am daylight
has erased it from the sky.
In all directions, the blue dome
reaches down to the roofs with their statues.

BULL HEART

**The bull-gargoyle
considers Europa's
effect on his heart.**

You're always heaving the windows open.
always running the furnace low.
The roses last beyond lifetimes.

A strawberry on the counter
is a concentrated blood star.
For all that, you trail Caucasian hillsides—

burnt olives and amber wine.
When I think of you skipping, when I sense
your meander, I cannot charge slowly enough

to freeze the dream, nor light
matches fast enough to immolate my heart,
which is so blown up now it holds a vat of vodka

and all of your spine bones and generators.
Wasn't it the god, my love, who fitted out
my chambers to hold you?

The atria could kiss your blue ears on top,
while the ventricles are a floor
for your little stomping snow boots,

The winds in the blood
flatten a trail that runs high and gleaming
toward an all-swallowing sunrise. See how it heats

and gives, gives and beats. See how
it shivers at the sight of your heart
light as a smile on glass.

Yevgeny's music

1.

**Longings of the
robot arm**.

The untuned may be in tune by chance, remain in tune,
a hand among starlings,
yet hard as a saucepan, or boinging like bedsprings,

lean and clean as a staple in a finger,
periodic as a pick, point-first on rock.

I might have been mush, a many-eyed potato
sunk in thickish loam,
or tumbling, wave-flung, ceaseless gravel,
or soursalt that sweetens a glass of tea.

Yet I must be Yevgeny, like a fork stabbing flank,
but gladder, gentler, more generously
desperate, slapping at my telos
among the smooth stones.

2.

O gullets craving knowledge, acid and bubble!
They desire cooked beet root, blood, baked apple.

How secret, aimless, is the life of the dying.

The sky's alight with jagged tendon
that no one sung or cast in wax.
Soon by night there is chanting at our backs.

Yet I want all my alloys to come alive
though they scream in every unoiled hinge,
though armor purples when ax hacks vein,
though all my silicon sizzles.

Can't my hand tear summer lutes by the strings?
Won't heaven sing through me as if my million holes
could strain out all clumsiness and longing—
in tune with the sun-trounced moon?

Yevgeny the robot
arm is taken from
the Radium Institute
in St. Petersburg to
work on scientific
projects at an
Antarctic station;
the reaction of his
lover, Lyuba, who
works at Taurus's
dance club and in
his watch business.

One day Yevgeny did not return to the Club.
Lyuba, distraught, could barely move,
her robot body, so lithe and smooth,

hitched and balked, as if crossing ruts.
The radium janitor had no answers.
"The next day, gone."

Taurus could not explain it
until the photos began to come.
The slave Yevgeny had been ripped from his laboratory,

shipped to Ukrainian Antarctic Station
"Academician Vernadsky."
Nothing the bosses did could keep out the cold.

Yevgeny's longing for Lyuba
almost could not be borne,
and yet the work was not bad—it was always dark.

Auroral angels gilded polar night.
He studied energy transfer of man-caused disturbances
from the surface of Earth to geospace height,

and measured the magnetosphere's micropulsations
in the Antarctic's magnetic climate,
measured energy channels

from Vernadsky to Boston,
and manmade electromagnetic noise,
gradients of warming waters,

the spreading-crack ice, the eloquent rasp
of chinstrap penguins, velocity of krill.
He discoursed with whales about the frontiers of life

He'd keep details in a diary, would write her
when he could. And when the winter was over,
he'd measure cesium 137 in men.

and when spring came, and daylight
briefly returned, he'd think only of his Lyuba,
And when they'd given papers

at the next Vernadsky conference in Russia,
he would come to her at night,
he would marry her by day.

She would join him among blue icebergs,
cathedrals past the melting point,
where they'd sink before parting again.

Taurus gave Lyuba a little space,
access to a keyboard, a flat screen, a toggle
that could block Yevgeny's e-mail,

but she wrote and wrote him,
like a blue-white wave
overwhelming an eons-old glacier.

It was then she revealed
she'd visited the warehouse.
She'd brought along a spring

she'd taken from Yevgeny's shoulder,
and there, on the platform
where robots made watches, she had removed

tiny gears from her redundant servo,
and made a watch using stable cesium
that resonated to the spheres.

And she would bring it to Yevgeny,
with its little hands,
and they could teach those hands

to pour and spill and mend,
to dance the ballet
of matter-in-time.

BALL LIGHTNING

*God is day and night, winter and summer, war and peace, surfeit and hunger;
but he takes various shapes, just as fire, when it is mingled with spices, is named
according to the savor of each.*

*   *   *

*This world, which is the same for all, no one of gods or men has made. But it
always was, is, and will be an ever-living Fire, with measures of it kindling, and
measures going out.*

Heraclitus

On Nevsky by the Dom Knigi renovation,
Taurus jeers at the titans on the deco dome top
who muscle up a glassy globe
placed there by Singer Sewing Machine.

Below, cross-legged on pavement, a streetsinger
beats time on a head-shaped drum,
hollow, with a rounded tone.
Like the god's voice, but without the god.

Without even the demigod, the hemidemisemigod.
The bull-man, revved up, ready to explode—listens:
That rhythm? Is it an empire falling?
Is that glass kniving into Nevsky tar?

The canal today blue and smooth as Iznik tile.
Heaven knows why this weary-looking man
has dropped a handline
into the globe's reflection,

rippling it. The water settles, then explodes.
A carp flaps on the embankment
breathing air. Everything's
waiting to be caught. The god is here.

Appearance from lightning strike on soil

I. E. Gortunov (male), programmer, engineer. 14 years old, July 1952.
Interview 1997. Daytime. Village, Enishevo of Smolenskaya oblast,
Russia.

Boys and I were fishing. A black cloud approached and a thunderstorm began.
We hid in the wooden building of a mill, in the pole basement. A bright
flash broke out during strong rain and the broken trajectory of a linear
lightning suddenly appeared. It struck into the body of the earthen dam.
Simultaneously I felt a strong electric shock into my bare feet. In spite
of this, I detected a blinding ball of the size of an orange fruit ascending
into the air 20 m from me, originating from the place where the linear
lightning struck. It was of red colour, like the colour of a ruby laser; and
irradiated more intensely than an incandescent lamp of 200 W. Its clear-
cut surface was well seen. The ball was hissing and slightly crackling. It
got to a height of 3−4 m by flying over an arc in length about 10 m with a
speed about 1 m s−1, descended to the ground, and exploded. Its sound was
like a cannon shot. Totally, it lived for about 15 s. After the thunderstorm
we investigated the place of the linear lightning strike, and found a crater
of about 70 mm diameter and a corkscrew dip. We could not detect the place
of the ball lightning explosion.

There are grooves and dips on earth where the god walked.
Fruits of the god, and heats, and freezes.
Can the god be brought down into black ceramic?
Can the god be crazing on fired mud? Will he break
like a dam? Will ichor scour the mounds?

Tonight, even moths cannot sleep.
Their painted wings quake from too much flapping.
They land on sticky silk, and none go free.
In the arachnosphere, hopes belong to the spider.
The god is cobwebs on a vase, windtraps in the stratosphere.

The god in wait, and nothing can elude him.
In pursuit, and none will match his speed. .
No, lovers, no one outflies the god.
Who else may bleed the earth, may trap the blood
in a brazier and cook it till it strikes like a snake?

Light shoots point to point across the soul,
and this bullet too is god. Nets brush
in a network. Hearts meet and tear—
like clay pounded together, pulled taut, they break.
Your breath catches in the back of my throat

like a hook. It is your mortal breath,
the breath of circuses and war, but what is all
your violence to a god? This is how he forms you,
geosphere, biosphere. He beats you like clay.
You crackle. The god is here.

Penetration through a windowpane, penetration into electric outlet

M. I. Oleneva (female) a pensioner. Observation 1955, a letter with description 1990. Reaction—fear. City, Kstovo near Nizhnii Novgorod, Russia.

It was gloomy before raining, but with no thunderstorm. My son, my mother and I were sitting by the table. The table was covered with an oilcloth. A small windowpane was opened by 100 mm. A fireball rolled through this space. It was very slightly yellow. We were all scared and did not move. A white electric outlet made of china was 0.5 m from us. The ball began to crawl inside this through one of the two holes. It almost all entered into the outlet, but the tail, the last part of the ball, was drawn into the other hole. Then a strong explosion was heard. A fire and a lot of soot appeared. The electric outlet was broken into pieces and its parts became black.

Taurus's horned head begins to pulse.
Everywhere are hints of balls and spheres:
Camel humps, articulated shoulder,
semicircle moon, an almost round grave,
a woman's peaking breasts, arch of agitated cats,
a robin-pecked worm, balling up,
a robot at the bottom of the sphere of the world
measuring a sphere of heat uprising.
Its lover robot, on a great circle plane, geolocates him.

On an ordinary day, the body celestial
electrifies the eye, floating music remembered.
Banded planets, neutron stars.
Ping. Ping. They fire at our sensors,
perturbing magnets, straightening hair.

In what sphere is Taurus? Unpopulated light?
An endless, parched darkness, an intergalactic No?
He charges a market's open-air booths,
rips at a palace's red-berry bushes,
spits balls of foam at the bronze chizhik pyzhik.
They hit the bird's feet. They don't slide
into the river—will he have luck for a 1000 years?

A nightingale loses its song inside its beak.
Ravens claw at a round mole, shredding.
Treebuds open out from the center of all growing.
Fluff explodes in fusillades.
Horizons twist, wrench apart.

Soul crosses into soul, borders popping.
Every god, every demon, every being has a sphere,
every second, every animal breath of air.
In a glass, water has a spherical cap.

Drink, bull-man. Ride the blue cloudspider.
Europa drinks from the same web of waters.
Bright balls burst. The god is here.

Swaying soap bubble that was broken into uneven pieces

V. N. Nezamaikin (male) a student engineer. 20 years old, the end of June 1972. Interview 1992. Settlement Kopos, Ukraine.

In the morning I went hunting to a shore of the Dnieper river. The sky was clean, with no thunderstorm or precipitation. I came to an open place on the high shore of the Dnieper and noticed a luminescent object 7 m from me in the reeds. It was a ball of 100 mm diameter, of a bright blue colour. It radiated light like an incandescent lamp of 100–200 W. Its matter, dense in appearance, was swaying, also resembling a soap bubble. The ball stayed motionless in the air, 600–700 mm above the grass. Not thinking for long, I made a shot into it with my shotgun. The bullet consisted of lead pellets. The ball's size increased by 1.5 times, and after that it decayed with a bang. It broke into uneven pieces. They dissipated and then disappeared near the surface of the water. The whole event lasted for 1–1.5 min.

Struck, we see. Seeing, we shriek. Shrieking, we root, blossom, die.

The thunderbolt steers all things.

Our messages shower and zip in the blankness.

The god in the cobwebs catches and gathers them.

And feeds on them where no one can come near.

O ghost-pulses, ghost memories, absorbed forgettings.

Nothing left of us but song. The god is here.

Cotton-wool structure, unfortunate case

V. A. Rantsev-Kartinov (male) PhD in physics. 5 years old, autumn,
20:00 h, 1944. Interview 2000. Number of observers: 8. Settlement,
Kupino near Novosibirsk, Russia.

A rain ended. There was no thunderstorm. It was quiet with no wind, and hot
and stuffy.

I observed this event outdoors at a distance of 30 m from the object.
A woman went out from the house to fan a flatiron. I noticed a glowing ball
at a distance of 2–3 m from her. It resembled a cotton–wool ball of fist
size, 70–90 mm. When the woman put her hand with the flatiron behind her
neck, the ball flew into the iron. Before this, the ball was moving after the
iron. The observation time was 1–2 s.

The woman fell on the ground. People took her and buried her (head
out) in the ground (the traditional treatment for lightning strike victims).
After 0.5 h her face turned blue and she died.

Somewhere in metal memory, a forest.
Taurus's minerals came from there,
copper, tin, arsenic the hardener.

The limping blacksmith melted them all
and poured red metal into a mold,
cooled it, filed it, hammered layers till it rang.

Took it to a hill to check its conductivity,
left it out in lightning.
It came into its own. The current

seized it like a spider net,
but it came out stronger—
in free electrons, in flow like water, in heat

like an animal, in light like the boulevards,
in speed like the Metro, in waves like the Baltic,
in longing for women, in love

for Europa, in the vacuum of love,
pressure cooker love, the love
that mixes and turns the troposphere,

love that electrifies
the music of the spheres,
her innocent look when clouds

pass over—her sky-blue look
even as clouds pass—
Be it so. "The god is here."

Woolen-type structure, burnt grass

M. V. Lozovsky (male) a student. 8 years old, summer 1983-1984.
Interview 1994. Settlement Voronovo 40 km from Moscow, Russia.

It was at 17:00−17:30 h, and a strong thunderstorm broke out with a rain shower. There was a strong wind with air temperature 22−23 Celsius. My grandmother and I were returning from the forest. Suddenly we noticed a ball 200−220 mm in diameter in a round clearing 15 m from us. It was rolling with a spiral trajectory. The ball was rotating, touched the ground and made a movement for 50 mm. It resembled a tangle of woollen threads, as if blue threads covered a warp of red threads. The intensity of its radiation could be compared with an incandescent lamp of 120 W. We were scared and quickly went away. The next day we saw that the surface of the clearing was burnt out, so that its colour became brown−black.

The babushkasphere visits everyone by night.

It cleans the brainwebs with vinegar. It brightens the brain like birch.

The brain must be strong for beauty. This the grandmothers know.

Cherries fall. Men and bulls brighten for Europa.

Europa brightens like birch. Taurus thinks of nothing else.

He thinks only of cherries and her brightness.

He must squeeze her. He must read by her light.

He must breathe the bubbles of her atmosphere. The god is here.

Several objects, appearance from nowhere,
separation of one object into 6-7, decay into three shell-type pieces
and several small pomegranate grain-like pieces

A. S. Timoshuk (male), associate professor in chemistry. 6 years old,
April 1946. Interview 1990. City, Belaya Tserkov near Kiev, Ukraine.

It was 10:00−11:00 h in the morning at the end of April. It was the beginning of a thunderstorm: a thunderstorm cloud was approaching very quickly, and thunder broke out. A branching linear lightning shorted wires, going from a wooden telegraph pole to the other side of the street and over a broken branch of an old poplar. The distance between the objects and me was about 25 m.

At the moment of the shorting of the wires a yellow−green flash appeared near the upper insulator on the telegraph pole, resembling the intensity of a flash of electric welding. Inside of it grew a white ball about 150 mm in diameter. It slowly rolled over the inclined wire, increasing its velocity, changed to the colour of melted red metal, and during rotation provided many sparks. The ball was perceived as light in weight but not a hollow formation. At the lowest point of the wire it jumped to a lower wire 5 m from the pole. At the lowest point of this wire it fell down to the poplar branch, covering the distance of 0.5−0.8 m between them. At the moment of touching a strong crack sound was heard. The branch was broken and inclined. The ball decreased in size, but 6−7 balls of 40−60 mm diameter appeared, running over the branches. Then they expired simultaneously.

Approximately 3 s later a new ball of 120 mm diameter appeared from 'nowhere'. The place of its origin was 1 m to the right of the place of formation of the first ball. It moved over the inclined thick branch, accelerating, smoothly and elastically jumping over any unevenness. It decreased to 90–100 mm, spreading many sparks. Then it jumped onto the roadway, where it jumped in a similar fashion to a gas balloon. The heights of its jumps were 200, 120 and 50 mm; in so doing the amplitudes decreased, but the frequency of jumps increased. Then the ball decayed into three big pieces of a shell shape and several further smaller pieces. The collection resembled a broken pomegranate with red grains on the ground. The destruction of the ball was viscous, similar to snow rolled-up into a snowball, whose structure is laminated. Parts disappeared non-simultaneously. Total duration of the event was 18–20 s.

So many spheres: Alpha-beta rains from a radium strip,

microballoons in radiation-slurping slurry,

a fist severed from its arm in a museum of curiosities,

the magnetosphere's Antarctic fluxion.

The god floating down from the deosphere,

balls of Uranus in the sea and Aphrodite,

the amorosphere with its transports, its landings

on a gravelly runway over permafrost melting,

on a stage in an opera where the sound of Italian

reminds the audience of falling water, and everyone leaves just dead.

Round emergences, curved convergences,

gradual bend of longitude and latitude,

right ascension, declination, in celestial navigation,

the telosphere to which all actions tend,

the dynosphere through which all movements arc,

the arcosphere in which all space

is a row of Soviet-style dwellings

before the solo volcanos of Petropavlovsk,

and whole armies of grandmothers come to market

with vats of round pink salmon eggs more plentiful than stars.

The dumposphere overfilled with garbage of the oblasts,

the credosphere of gullible tendencies,

the terpsichosphere where everyone dances with the god.

All wave arms, lock hands, hear trains.

Tie-rhythm, wheel-beat, humming near.

Out of nowhere, the god is here.

Appearance from nowhere, large size, soft bubble, interaction with observers

T. S. Sychevskaya (female) a teacher of pre-school. 17 years old,
20:00 h, June 1971. Interview 1998. 5 observers. City, Zapadnaya
Dvina, Russia.

In the evening my friends and I went to a dance. It was rather cool after a thunderstorm, but with no wind. We crossed the Moscow—Riga railway. We just had crossed the rails and suddenly noticed a spherical ball lightning over our heads. It was of 700–800 mm diameter. It appeared as if from nowhere. We got frightened, squatted, and connected our hands, creating a circle. The ball suddenly began to move over us in a circle, and it also moved up and down. It was at a height of 0.5 m above the ground. Then it 'chose' my head and began to jump on it, up and down, like a ball. It made more than 20 jumps. It was as soft as a bubble and I did not even feel its weight. I felt cold from it. The ball resembled a gel of white–grey colour. Its boundary was like a soap bubble. Its glow could be compared with that of an incandescent lamp of 200 W. Inside the ball (at 1/3 of its diameter) the glow was more intense than outside. Then it ascended and disappeared unexpectedly. After this contact we were throwing up.

Sphere of the individual, everyone unique,

the collectivity—uniqueness in all,

sphere nichovo ne znayu, where nothing is known,

BBs in Kalashnikov BB rifles,

a golf ball a cosmonaut drove into orbit,

the spheres of grease in sorrel soup,

concentric spheres of an infinite regression

to ever-smaller personal divisions.

Taurus in a sphere of uncontrolled creation,

his head in poplar tangles bobbing on a windless day,

a garble of spherical poplar seed planets.

In what sphere is Europa with her elegance and ease?

Will poplars reach the roundness

of her eyes? Will they touch her tongue,

change all to one? The god is here.

Vibrating gel, thinness of the sacred—

anyone can break it with a spit or a sigh.

Awake, we see only death. In slumber, only sleep.

But for a moment, the sea may be clear as it is deep.

Curve of the return when no line goes there,

return of the curve where only lines had been,

interconnection—orbits, braincanals,

gravitic tunnels from Earth to Mars or Venus,

gods in a tree, goddesses in mushrooms.

Fluff skims a river. Something bursts.

Sound floats across the brain like a distant ship.

It runs like golden rain through the temporal lobe,

triggers a glimpse of Love, smell of sliced pear,

unannounced, a heaven. The god is there.

Radiant, love in circumnavigations,
circumlocutions, circumambulations.

There is a thunderstorm. No thunderstorm.
Tree. Or none.

Love's a ball.
We're balancing bears. Someone's

always about to fall.
The rain is always

raining till it's done,
until it rains again.

A bounce like a plectrum
across the branches.

In each moment, a Europa
or an ending.

Something bursts.
The god is here.

MESSAGES FROM THE GOD

1.   Dei/logue

The god inhabiting
the bull-gargoyle
practices speeches
to Europa as the
bull listens.

The god will not shut up:
"History ends in piles and husks.
Storms white, storms black, earth gone.

Everywhere, earth is gone.
Railroads arrow from the steppe's end through far villages.
Men throttle chickens, trample fields,

trade bombs for apples, and apples for bombs.
as if some other earth—a green-bottle eye—
will rise over the taiga.

But there is no such earth. We inherited no other.
Black wave, black wave breaking with a white,
exhaustions of soot and snow.

Our design is—things run out.
Thus the steppe scrub hunkers low,
and sleepy sheep mill in spirals, converging.

What's more unmoored than a droop-eyed god?
Tired from too much sleeping, I would like
a nap. On goose-down cushion,

to count waves on a lake, from a cloud room
to glide over warrior nicks and hacks,
and to dream from the beginning

through the slow monotonies of the ticking world,
till my dream comes to you,
my sweet sweet you,

as if you were the first and brightest ray of moon
to play green-stalk lyres
in budded fields.

Light is the purest antidote to woe,
cutting through grain,
spewing from a girl.

Even to a god who snorts and snores,
the light is warm. It strikes the ore of shadows,
and even a god is warmed."

2.   **Bull/china**

The bull-gargoyle's
reaction to the
god's rehearsal.

The warm ax-head voice
hits Taurus behind the eyes, drowsying the bull.
Horns drop into a bowl,

splattering an archipelago of sour cream
halfway to Finland,
or just blebbing the warped linoleum

as coffee steams up from his espresso cup
in a mocking cloud, like a mock-up of the god,
fogging the basement café

where card tables
lurch out of kilter
when touched by a fork or news—

as if gravity were constantly lumping, shifting,
in the changing magnetics
of kettle and plate,

unsettled by divine agitations—
The god zeroed on the girl, the multiplying zeros
bleb upon bleb almost reaching her.

Taurus twitches
in a coffee-breeze.
The china rocks as he moos.

3.   Distance

The god tries out
another speech to
Europa; distinctions
between human
and god.

"Europa, my apple, look at your kind.
Every cell breaks, or wears to little heaps.
All of your waters rush out, pooling,

all of your pools go cement-gray and steam
in shavings, urine, swampgas, wind.
Man's a heap of cells who fires little lightnings,

But the greater lightning accumulates in gods
who beautify or foul, as case may be,
rainwater, floodwater, salt-sweat sea

with electric muscularity.
We shock the sceptre from an emperor's hand
and prod some child to use it for a bludgeon.

It needles through blue beads
to add another necklace to the empire—till we tire
and ocean salts the sceptre.

Wars go on in the aftermath of war
as a flood piles wave over wave on barren rock.
Sad earth, sorry earth, drools and bawls.

Her ancient skin chafes like the skin of a newborn,
tongue-tied and toothless, in a shroud of cloud.
These aren't our wars, nor she our mother.

Our battles rage beyond bliss or erosion.
We roam radiant banks of sun-bloody bays
and scheme for our hybrids and concubines.

Immortality alone betrays us. We never lie down
in the green stalk land, nor skip stones,
nor yield to moon-scarred flows.

And therefore I crave the mortal gush.
In a breathing hide, I charm you in a pasture
till puffballs blacken the summer soil."

4. Block out

An interrupted
reverie.

Staring down the coffee's black,
the bull drops into his own thoughts.
Dandelions yellow the sad little lawn on a concrete island.

They send olfactory contrails
that brush him with desire
cut by crankcase oil and smoke.

"The god's not entering my thoughts at all," thinks Taurus,
thrilled in a dream of crossing—
at a canter to dare buses to dent him.

Down he'll bend and smear nose with pollen.
Taut lips will yank sweet plants by the roots
and toss them, and catch.

Tongue will indulge in a mash of prickly leaves,
a pleasure he normally shuns
in the presence of a girl or god.

The god! The shouting, headlong as a train—
Europa, Europa, how much *Europa*! The bull
waves down the waitress for his check.

5.   Among the mortals

The god encourages
Europa to see herself
as chosen.

"O earth, domain of wet-haired men
whose walkways are cracking, whose foundations craze.
Fates faultline through their days.

But in the end, one. I say, 'Die,' and they do.
If I say so or not, they die, in fact.
Like dandelions, newts, the blind rosy moles.

Did we promise more
than a nailscratch in clay
the summer rain would smooth away?

Or that their lyres and combs
would hang like butterflies in velvet,
or we'd make mementos

of their falling flesh,
in swan, seamonster, snakes, a girl,
mere outline, yet flint for memory?

A few we favor. We assume a form,
no longer zing about, but breathe,
shed the awesome shapelessness of power,

and hay pokes us. We shake off dew
as moonlight needles through leaves of an oak.
For a second, every air is new:

the barred owl's barking so the fieldmice quake,
an army lazing by aspens, basking in flares,
half-dead and half-awake.

And we spume a chosen mortal
like a gale across a lake
that had only heard of gales from veering seabirds."

6.   Intercourse

The god rehearses   "Be water to my wind. Come, reddened as a flare.
how he will implore   Bring earth's charms
Europa to approach.   to the cloud-curtained god

till dead sun burns up golden doves,
and seasalt cures the boiled egg soul.
Bring timeless gasps till you grow cold, and I go on.

Till you're calm, though sky's an inkblot,
though Heaven is noise,
and human and god still dream of each other

traveling tracks through barely touching trees.
A railway shoots. A city falls toward dawn.
The sediment thickens, more perfect for dreams.

And I dream of you, my apple, my pulsar.
O blue-shifting whistle,
bring light back to me."

7.   Temples

Taurus's headache; the pharmacy; his own thoughts of Europa.

The god is a threnody in Taurus's brainpan.
On the stage-set of his brainpan,
the god has the lines.

How does His Antiquity hope to win her?
By train wheels
wheezing more rust than steel?

Taurus pounds the concrete
from café to pharmacy.
The cashier line undulates through the store

and back to beginning—head-eating-tail.
At the booth he asks for aspirin
"and something to keep me awake."

His insides already coffee bean lava.
Head about to hatch
into a million copper worms,

to link with the deepest bottom of some White Sea.
He likes to peer down dark
to see if darkness looks back.

So today, all he discerns of Europa
are the green-black feathers of the greener depths
where odd life dangles bulbs. His questing eyes

touch a ring of tentacles in muted light.
The soft-mouthed sea flower gulps—eyes gone. . . .
The pharmacist, looking at him quizzically,

has arrayed the bull's relief
in a pyramid of boxes and vials, receipt on top,
like an altar for knife and animal.

8.   Fertilizer

The god shifts to a
monologue on his
own mortality; **a**
storehouse of
discarded gods;
thoughts of fertility.

"Forgotten before I was banned— a congeries of marble
in a dank museum basement, arm touching leg.
You could not tell my brother's nose

from my crumbling thumb.
Then within four small walls,
a thousand gods more were dumped into the pile,

and those who did the dumping
were dumped on our backs, decades of clatter and shatter.
Ice crystals in winter. Window sweat in summer.

A weed or two grew like liberation from the floor,
cracked cement shaken by tanks and artillery.
The mounting count of gods

from every flat space of the realm,
from every tall mountain and windy plateau,
from tribes of desultory sheep

113

that had split off from the herd
and made temples of tufts and tumuli.
Fleece gods, then, and toothed and hooved,

who had taught games of chance
to any who would listen, but now—
pricked with pentothal through the tongue,

could only say, "We won't last a week or two."
What crops could grow in powdery marble?
Cellars, dismal rooms, the rage that burns them,

that smell of burning hair and starving skin.
Jaws and hips of children pulverized in factories,
painted into houses, smeared by mimes.

All beside the point, the fate of bulls, men, or gods:
Whom to strike down?
Whom to save?

All beside the point. Only water, loam, and bone,
sperm filling the fracture lines of clay—
seed craving holy sun."

9.   Such gifts

**Taurus lurches out
into the city.**

A forsaken park. The bull-man pauses to breathe.
As a white flock ravages a tiny patch of grass,
Taurus can already smell the river.

He smells waterbugs and gnats,
whose careless tracks
leave scarcely a ripple where currents roll.

He too feels hardshelled, barely noticed
trudging tank-like through St. Petersburg,
past sputtering carburetors, Vespas and Planetas,

Taurus—"driver" to the talking fireball,
who rattles and wheedles
and hoots for Europa.

10.   Ochi chernya

The god desires
Europa's dark,
mortal eyes.

"So many armies, so many icy floors.
The boot-ground wheat grains
loll in muck.

Leather torn from a horse
ties a shoulder to an arm.
The glorious resourcefulness

of humans as they fall
with every face of bliss or oblivion!
Earthworms

vacuum their blackened eyes,
widening the pupils
like pots dug out for seed.

And you, my darling, leaf and stem,
thornapple, come
and grow in my sight,

grow fanatic
in my breath,
fill the flowerpots with light."

11.   Peter's walk

Out in the city,
near Hare Island,
the bull-gargoyle
thinks of a myth
of the city's founding,
multiplicity.

Flowerpots! The bull begins to shuffle
past a palace door framed by spindly roses—
wan, sparse leaves on the stem.

The pots have a firebird glazed into the clay
which seems about to fly away, faded as brown
as the waning blooms.

The scent sends Taurus on a rotten sweet drunk.
He senses the peat on top of the pots,
like the island peat that Peter cut

and laid crosswise: *The city will be here.*
On a day he wasn't there, so Taurus is thinking.
Isn't history a day someone was there,

and not mere fluff that rides on air, scintillating everywhere
when the night comes fast as a sheet pulled taut
and snapped across your memory?

You stand in the street, watch the pied petals fall
out of time, or can't recall
what story you were telling in what habitation.

Droplets pull new smells from soil,
the smell of must, of rock and roll,
glass up the nose, black tobacco,

chemical reels of yellowed films moldering in official rooms
no one thinks to open. Eternal friction
brings you to yourself, dragging along a street

where once you hid your face, and now you walk
smelling attars of rain, bull nose tickled by fennel and fires
that burn in industrial memory.

And in the midst of all the snares and frauds,
the drowning thunder of the exasperating god,
it may be true: the city will be here, framing you against a wall.

Perhaps a woman's finger on the shutter
will flash the darkness, catch the bull
about to go full-tilt across a square

because the god is with you,
because you've never been so much yourself—
seen in a shop window,

doubled and redoubled,
or like a hologram, *en plein aire*,
because the god is all desiring, yet gives all.

12.   Capercaillie cock

The god implores
Europa through a
country dream.

You dream at the surface. Land meeting river.
Light meeting impenetrable river,
but only near the surface; only there.

Sedge and cranberries are bobbing up.
Shuffles of birch bark and bubbles touch the light.
Rock-torn marten fur floats in glare.

In your eyes, for long seconds, the surface is alive.
In your ears, for long seconds, you hear the capercaillie,
deaf to the world when it sings to its mate.

Only then can it be killed, when its song is all,
red-browed and fantailed, too stiff to fly.
Beak to the sky, the cock sings for your light.

From the boat of your dreams, Europa,
hear the capercaillie, tune surfacing,
submerging, resurfacing, till night.

13.   Genealogy

**The god practices
explaining himself
to Europa; his
origins; his
manifestations.**

It is a bad night. The god blabs on and on.
Lightning rages over the Neva.
Taurus notices a door in a Rostral Column

where no opening has been before.
He pulls the door. A stairway shimmers.
Now up and up the looming stairs,

trying to get the god out of his head.
"When my father tried to eat me,
mother fed him stone. For my name was stone,

and she hid me in mud. In the mud of great rivers,
she hid me in coffins
that floated downriver when ice broke in spring.

And I rose against him from the many-armed mud.
I killed him again and again."
Taurus moves one booted hoof, then the next.

Water rushing, rising up the column,
now at his ankles, now his knees.
"Therefore, I have only *more* to give—

frost around the moon, the innerness of trees,
over and over of dawning day,
obscuring air that twinkles a star

again and again and again.
I'm storm—repeats of shocks, winds, drops.
rattles of barrels in the heavens.

I'm time that feeds the flood,
and nothing is enough, and I give more and more,
and still there's more to give—

to bathe a waning earth, her cities winking out,
to pole a load of souls across a river of stars
to banks where they'll wait to be born."

14.   Flood/light

The flood whirls
the god; he looks
for Europa.

Taurus from a high step watches as the flood
rips the city's foundations.
Khruschev-era walls collapse, plow into a church.

The canals are thick with junk—scaffolding, paintcans,
a sculpted sunburst light of the divine,
a coconut painted with the face of Peter,

gilt replicas of Petersburg public art
from the era of Catherine to the Soviets' fall
swirling by the souvenir stalls.

"I whirl, spiral like a poplar seed,
linger like a poplar seed, sprout among piles.
I'm straining upward. Love confounds me.

120

Is that surface?
Is it sky?
Bring your light."

15.   Coda

Light comes in a breath,
and then gone,
thinks the bull.

Light dreams
in a breath, and it's
dream, dreams the god.

Light sings in
a breath, one
song, moos the girl.

The rain-cracked moon
pressed into a ball—for one
blink, whole.

DVD FROM EUROPA

The bull-gargoyle receives an animated message from Europa; a version of a Russian fairy tale.

Europa, in translucent fabrics, embraces a bull-man.
She in tears, his eyes ravines.
He must go, and says in his rumbling way:
do not leave the apartment, or heed evil words.

She checks her messages every day.
She has many correspondents.
Every day she writes of love.

Old Woman sends a message. Who is Old Woman?
"A walk in this garden will ease your grief."

Old Woman is so right. A walk
in a garden. Old Woman
has sent a virtual garden.
The ferns are tall. The flowers
have shapes of lion and fox.

Out goes Europa, strolls through the flowers.
A spring-fed pool extends clear, cool hands.
They hold a message: "Come in, come in."

Off slips her gown. She walks into the water.
Suddenly an old woman strikes her on the neck.

Europa, changed, is a white duck,
and the witch is now Europa, trying on her robe,
painting Europa's face on her own.
When the bull-man comes home, he does not know.

The white duck lays eggs in high, cold reeds.
Three hatchlings go exploring.
They stray near the apartment.
The false Europa knows them by their smell.

She turns on a burner.
Gas dizzies the chicks.
With the hard hand of a corpse
the crone beats and kills them all.

When the white duck finds her babies
(kerchief-white, minnow-cold),
she holds them with her wings and laments
in a voice that is almost Europa's.

Hearing, the bull-man chases after her in vain,
then finds the needed words:
"Birch behind, girl before."

Now a birch tree stands behind him, Europa before.
A magpie flies with seedpods
holding waters of life, of speech.
The waters pour. Chick skin shudders.
More waters pour, and the babies
tell the Old Woman's misdeeds.

Tied to a cloud, she's dragged by one leg.
Her logic goes barren as crow-ravaged corn.
Her cells fly off like hawk-hunted sparrows.

Finally, Europa, white-winged in woman's body,
and her feathered babies lift off.
They fly around the bull-man,
crying joy in ducky tongues,
their call still roughened
by the high, cold reeds.

The tableau ends. The screen blanks to silhouettes—
ducks like arrows—and
From your white duck, Europa.

FORGIVENESS

Europa to the bull. I haven't run at the night or slammed it down like you,
or swirled a darkness in the well of my eye
and gone drunk on it all day
in crushed cement cities. I settled in a smooth place,
among plans, pavers, graders, a square
where a girl could balance berries on her tongue.
When I dance, I keep my steps small.

I haven't lobbed stars into a sinkhole
or trucked in a thousand slaves' hands
to stack the boulders and shave the shale.
I won't lug palaces onto wheels
and pull them like horsecarts.
I believe in mercy as in a jackknife.
There's every imaginable instrument and blade.

I haven't killed or intended to kill,
but I'll sand the killing out of anyone's voicebox.
I haven't gored shadows in a gray-leaved garden
or trampled the percolating dead.
Yet in my mazy, blowing gown, I peel back
the gut-folds of a sheep or a bull
and filter fates in a colander of bone.

Your cracked hide won't stop me. No, never.
I'm a horse in full tilt through falling-down streets,
whinnying the oldest, maddest hymns.
I eat apple sauce mashed with a fossil egg
and haunt canals like a sleepless hag carrying beets
in a carpet bag knitted from bristles and thistles.
Those barbs could tear up a whale.

Could a girl put her hands into lava
to pull out mountains and count the litter?
I haven't pushed my head up through undulating thunder
and looked down to see war's fingernails.
Yet I believe in this creek that lips the fugitives' path.
Get low in its ice, and it blocks the gas fires
that rush us like ranks of dogs.

And you who will not yield even to ants
that jitter by, hoisting ribbed leaves of lettuce,
carrot peelings, garlic skins,
you the hardest element in the periodic table,
sly bull, who are yourself a mountain,
do not deny me, for I'm the next snow.
I will enter your eye, like a cave into a mountain.

Though I do not know the way,
I'll duck and crawl. I'll pull and stick and crawl
up to your tear ducts, and out in tears
into the crying world, like rain hits a spring slope
onto white ribs curved like beached boats.
The names of the nameless are dripping from god's lips
in the joy and spit of his forgiveness.

Vapors: dawn

1.   Ur-cloud

**The bull-gargoyle's
message to the
model Europa; to
meet her in
St. Petersburg under
the constellation
Taurus during
White Nights.**

In the all ever-seething, don't we all seethe as one?
Since all started as one, don't I feel you
quicken, even a continent away?

Steam boils out of star-born kettles.
It might be mousebreath or ghostliness of manholes,
might be a bombsplash, or ancient lace

conjured on a humid stroll
by grayed-out city waters,
by the Church Over Spilled Blood.

2.   Far away near

Distance is injury. And so, my darling,
I look for you here, on the far side of time,
on my Russian streetcorner.

Not knowing where you are, I look up at night,
the just-past-dusk that passes for darkness,
where the dead meet mainly the dead.

Not knowing, I scan screens—
bull-faced, bull-intentioned—
breathing mainly delirium.

3.   Anyone, anywhere

I'll meet you anywhere elements are forming,
any year by a skin-chewing sky,
where beacons gore the scintillating dark,

and sleepers follow lights as if led by a god,
only to wake in bric-a-brac—
foundered memories, bladed moons.

We'll meet where anyone met before,
we who were nothing but wounds before,
aches in astringent waves.

Come, love, we'll flop in all the rainbows.
The sun passing through us
will tell what's to be.

4.   Once in Tyre

Remember, near Tyre, l came to you.
Though all the mist-crazed girls stopped to gape,
I was calm and warm and slow.

You ran fingers down my flank as down a map—
finding outlines of battlements, and shady arcades
in a ruin the gods had scoared there,

and bodies fractured, fallen on rocks,
before bulls knew pens or gods had names.
Moist and barefoot on a ledge, you traced my hide.
I thrust my head into wet brush,
pulled out hanks of heal-all.
You trembled like wind across a pool.

5.   Signs

Now cellphone billboards everywhere
beam that we're no longer creatures
of the earth, and so I look for you in canals,

among caryatids and statues,
on the back of gold-winged gryphons
whose mouths hold up the footbridge. . .

What frenzy could be more tempting
than the hazy slipper of the Pleiades,
barely glinting in your sign?
Let our signs join. A bull can deliver
hoof sparks, hot breath, tongue huge as a god's,
a rod that can shiver seas.

6.   Crash

Let's lie upon each other like two tattoos,
the scene of a crash in stifling summer.
We'll boil off the ink and marinate the scars

in vodka, rubbing alcohol, and entrepreneurial ventures,
flasks that taste of horseradish and woodland fruits,
deposits of salts from half-gloved hands,
some yours, some mine, flying over balalaikas.
Though we are destinies apart, we'll see the city plain—
the entrances, the exits, the ticket sellers.

7.   Healed

A herd of ambulances, crossing Fontanka,
splatters iron hides of the bridge's black steeds.
They glisten with the pathos of eternal stars

that gleam for the angry pleasure of gleaming,
when keyboards are a rage of rain.
Do wounds ever join? Geography is pain.

There's a scratch on your cornea the shape of a bay.
My cheek's livid with squeezings of bilberries.
Let's out-heal any miracle before,

you here, and I here, and a rained-over moon
and vans reviving their deliveries.
Then we'll climb from one red ocean, out of time.

BAKERY

1.

**Europa imagines
the bull-gargoyle
will abandon her,
and she'll work
in a bakery.**

All that was— veins without the leaf,
crust and crumb scorched black,
courtyard soot and frost and soot.

Look! A million birds in the apple tree.
They've no interest in bread.
They puncture tiny apples.

I sweep the punctured skins. I sing a punctured song.
Why do I slump,
folded over, and cold?

2.

**She addresses the
bull-gargoyle; her
dreams.**

Perhaps, beast, you did not know old women dream,
and truth gave bone to dreams
long before I dreamt of you.

Did you drain my every fate
except to wait, except to wait,
and sweep the waiting into piles

and tip the waiting down a can
and stir it in the can with rain
until it's time to wait again?

No. I watch the bakery's TV.
I look for lightning on the maps, and hatless rush outside
and try to drink you down.

To catch you on my tongue
and swig you till you're gone. Then bolts move past.
No droplet drums. Alone,

I moan into my washing pail.
Breath makes patterns, rise and fall,
in suds and apple scums.

3.

She recalls the
bull-gargoyle.

I was from everywhere, from nowhere, sought by all,
and when the bull approached,
from searing dusk,

awesome as a vessel transported from a temple,
I (who believed most
in phosphorous, in matches—

the blue, the snap, the risk of extinction,
the cigarettes that kept me thin,
buds unfurling orange, the book erupting)

I lit like holy oil, and everywhere
went bright,
even smoke from his heaving sides.

4.

**Their lights
intermingling.**

Then I was on a hill facing a bull,
naked and near,
and I almost fainted.

Lamps—girl and bull—
rays interlaced like hands,
a lattice nothing could break,

though the day was black-sleek
and sky was a flash
hitting vessels and humors,

among minerals and smog,
only I and you
and the horizons.

5.

Europa's present.

Now the bonds of my molecules fray and give way,
and you do nothing, bull,
harrower, discarder.

Though I sweep through apples, wrappers, crusts,
breaks in this bakery's knobby breads,
apple pirozhki tender in the center,

as I was once,
now a bug broomed
in char from an oven,

faithful today as a bug to her god,
as god to his scatterings, as you to Europa,
faithful as I to my broom.

6.

**Her mind jittery
as a flour beetle**.
My thoughts blow like flour over flour,
erasing the footsteps
of *tribolium confusum*.

I can hardly remember the glint of your neck
when I leaned to kiss your back and felt my depths
roll across your hide.

I can keep track of nothing now.
I forget why this baker's teasing
torments me,

smiling in malice or pity as I stumble,
expression fuzzy though five feet away
while I rest on a garbage can,

boots gonging
under a shifting, brownish
cloud of starlings.

7.

Recalling their union.

You sounded like that gong
against my knuckles,
bovine heaver, bulbous twitcher,

when I pounded you from below,
your bulk suspended
as if the heat of Furnace Earth held it fixed there

while I shouted—
I can't remember if in pain or pleasure—
that a creature so cumbrous

could be cajoled to ring
by soft fists' battering
like rain on a dome,

like fruit swinging ravaged
by songbird beaks,
the interruptions of wings.

8.

She imagines him now.

Where are you now?
Do you lean from a cantilevered roof,
as if about to somersault off and chase a wren?

Or crouch in a niche
above a gold-green door,
horns poking curved beyond your shoulders?

The lean that leaned me,
horns that curved me,
to adore your force and ceremony?

You do not visit now.
You've hurled me down like bent coins
bearing the trenched face

of an exiled concubine,
who used to sway through
the very thresholds

where you perched high, an unblinking guardian.
Had a prince seen you blinking,
would he have let you in?

9.

His horns.   I let you in. A girl-flower let you in.
A meadowsweet ablush at things
that humans do to bulls,

heedless that your horns were milled for goring.
In the end, we were horn-mad.
You struck wall. Struck heart,

my mortar giving in.
Your horns abrading red sparks.
Till red went dark.

10.

Words find her.   When you bellow, the churches and motorcycles
tremble. Europa's voice has never
moved a hair on any head.

Yet words come to me like starlings.
One by one, beaks pierce red bubbles;
one by one, they swallow tear-shaped seeds

on afternoons when I pull every gown from every drawer
and try them out, and flush because they fit,
because I'm even smaller than I was before,

and I dazzle the lightbulbs, and pirouette,
mouth witticisms and almost-prayers
for the nuzzlings of a gem-horned beast.

11.

In his absence.
Why, bull, have you left me now to live or die,
guideless through mists and quarries,
groping for a boundary?

I am shapeless and black.
On every street, I wear your shadow.
My dust blows over concrete like a million birds.

Won't you pity your little cloud of disarrays?
Won't you charge me through a decrepit doorway
splashing in a sluice of apples?

You have partaken.
You have tossed away.
I arch back my neck

and look for you zeroing down at my soul,
small as a seed, small as a crumb,
your glassy gaze upon my song of ashes.

BOREALIS

City

The bull to Europa.　　The god once built a city in my heart.

Or who else drained the starry, swampy brine?

Who hammered down the pylons of long pine?

The landfills and the lanes were soaked and bright.

Armloads of dung, a pecker's ratatat.

Now I'm sleepless in a lightning-withered night.

Wind reeks of gasoline and too much talk,

of whacks wedged into necks. I hump my back

and run at every net until I'm caught.

Is it rain will slaughter me or blessed luck?

If god's left hand once pistoned on my snout,

I still wait for his right. Mapless, I walk

on a shattered arch in reedy riverlands.

Let sands break sandhills down to smaller sands.

Wind-flowers: *anemone coronaria*

Let sands break sandhills down to smaller sands.
If I dig my knees a hole, the sand is sky.
Beige moonlit motes are spinning off my hands,
and now's a hot glass bubble in my eye
bending these hours into a honied lump—
kasha, nasturtiums, clover, gritty oats,
fermented hay that reeks midsummer damp.
There's moistened breath, and sand, and hard-hooved fits.
Here's kale and sand, and sand and honeysuckles.
And now the god, a hurricane of sand,
outscreaming sparrow flocks and barn-eave swallows,
hoists up my spinning soul. Old rasp, old wind,
may dragonflies and teeming ants come fling
anemones down to my reckoning.

Between

Anemones down to my reckoning;
vine-darkened, speckled roses; monk's hood leaves;
bog star collapsed in heaps. Can some bright wing
sweep down between our skull-sacks and the waves
of crawling shade? Between the clouds' brim and
the mole rat's murk, here's half a light-filled inch—
low pasture weeds, my spiky boulder-land.
I wedge an eye in there. I crunch the crunch
of sheaves in side to side work of a jaw.
Who knows if the work is mine or from the blue?
One raven's talon jabs another's caw.
You shout. I duck. You duck. I shout: *It's you?*
There's half an inch to shout in and to see
a god's long tendrils joining you to me.

Herd

A god's long tendrils joining you to me
drive green and knobby through the stockyard clay,
a mush roughened with sand and cell debris.
Why in god's grasp are so many thrown so low
a lintel beam seems distant as a star?
Hooves hit the earth. Green guts reverberate.
The gates are latched, or there never was a gate.
A blade's behind the chute behind the door.
But praise the blade. The god has joined us here
by our gazes, by the feet, upright or beast.
He says, "Sweet creatures, come. Come, and be blessed.
There's love in severing and light in glare."
This blur-dark god was brighter than a bomb
in our closed eyes when they slid out of the womb.

Mist

In our closed eyes, when they slid out of the womb,
already we agreed on names of clouds.
God's flock of terns was tearing at a loom.
God's cloth of vapor lay draped on the reeds.
Warehouse facades were pressing out like hulls,
when you, my cloud girl, crossing slippery stones,
and I, a bullock trotting among bulls,
both heard the bursts in seaside power lines.
The hours had fallen out of all the works,
the gears gone gap-toothed in their trains.
A few sleepers queued for loaves and small sardines.
You hurried off. A shower startled larks.
Drops tickled them to pipe and print the shore.
Then east dissolved. That first light flared no more.

Aurora

Then east dissolved. That first light flared no more.
Dissolves and flares are all that we deserve
who hide from lightning when it slants toward shore.
Yet I loomed after you, charged you with love
along the sloppy docks. You ran from me
and stopped and lingered like a wind
that does not know it's wind, and cannot see
it's dust, and I was hooves and horns and sand.
To me your shape was ballads on the bones.
To you I was a warship setting fires.
And it was never night. And you sang lines
the god had never plucked from tight-strung stars.
The sun-wind's curtain twisted dark past dawn—
your glance a warming, gaze aurora-green.

Archaeology

Your glance a warming, gaze aurora-green
across my farm-wild hide, across the bindings
now barely stitched and the hard, half-rotten sheen
of leather thumbed through chapters, past all endings.
One line can build a thousand city walls
or make the sheetrocks give and bedsprings bark.
Lightnings will smelt the past. Yet nothing pales
this beautiful time, and I've brought you an arc,
a clasp to close. I'm hammering it now—
though grasshoppers all die without a name,
a northern frost browns beet-greens down the row,
and I am old as bronze, whiter than lime.
Let this diadem be yours, let digging start.
The god once built a city in my heart.

NOTES

"Club Bill" was adapted from a schedule for Griboedova, a club in St. Petersburg.

Vernadsky quotations in "Vernadsky" were adapted from http://www-ssg.sr.unh.edu/preceptorial/ Summaries_2004/Vernadsky_Pap_ITru.html.

"Objects named after V. I. Vernadsky" was adapted from the list at http://www.tstu.ru/eng/kultur/ nauka/vernad/imena.htm.

All except the "Europa" sections of "His age: Any" were adapted from various websites containing personal advertisements from Russian women.

Ball lightning reports in "Ball lightning" were adapted from Abrahamson, Bychkov & Bychkov, "Recently Reported Sightings of Ball Lightning," *Phil. Trans. R. Soc. Lond.* A (2002) 360, 11-35.

"DVD from Europa" was adapted from *Russian Fairy Tales*, by A. N. Afanasyev.

PAUL NEMSER's poems have appeared in *Antioch Review*, *Barrow Street*, *Pequod*, *Poetry*, *TriQuarterly*, *Horizon*, *Fulcrum*, *Arion*, *Columbia: A Journal of Literature and Art*, *Raritan*, and *Redivider*, among other magazines. He is also co-translator of two books by Ukrainian poets: *Square of Angels* by Bodhan Ihor Antonych (Ardis, 1977) and *Orchard Lamps* by Ivan Drach (Sheep Meadow, 1978). He lives in Cambridge, MA.

CPSIA information can be obtained at www.ICGtesting.com
Printed in the USA
BVOW09s2232051016

464290BV00007B/68/P

9 780984 943951